A Fake Memoir

Poems

Peycho Kanev

Cyberwit.net
HIG 45 Kaushambi Kunj, Kalindipuram
Allahabad - 211011 (U.P.) India
http://www.cyberwit.net
Tel: +(91) 9415091004
E-mail: info@cyberwit.net

Contents

I

Manifesto

I grew up in Communism.
My grandmother and I were sitting in
the living room, in front of the TV,
watching the speech of the Chairman
of The Communist Party, with the rest
of the country.
The teeth of my grandma were grinding.
I asked: "What's the matter, granny?"
She sat there, quiet for a while, and
then she said: "This man should die.
I just hope someone to kill him!",
and after a few noiseless minutes
she told me: "If you, my boy, tell
someone what I've just told you
now, I will kill you!"
Then she smiled with her bad teeth,
but I noticed something in her eyes,
that made me silent, until now.

The Moment

The black steel. The blistered paint. The brownish dust.
The rust. The humming. The wires mixed up like wet
spider web. The yellow tape around. The hot, orange sun.
The lonely birds. The gentle breeze. The young man
approaching carefully. The heavy boots. The small, grey
rocks. The shrieking of the gods. The fear. The young man
leaning forward. The eyes and the sweat. The trembling
fingers. The heavy suit. The memories of the high-minded
knights. The helmet. The pliers. The uncertainty. The seconds.
The hesitation. The vacillation. The flash of the Gordian
knot. The silence. The bomb disposal robot. The mechanical
sound. The extending of the metallic arm. The heavy body.
The lifting. The seconds. The beads of sweat dripping from
the forehead. The jamming. The silence. The static in the radio.
The orders. The memories of home and the baby crib. The pliers.
The decision. The short prayer. The stillness. The moment.
The cut. The blast. The silence. The silence. The silence.

War

Hard Arabic light
falls
on the adobe hut

The little girl
in rags
begs for food
from the soldier
who
killed her mother

In-depth

And
inside this night
of monochromatic
light I see
my father stepping
further
in the clouds – but my fingers
reach to touch your place

   still warm two years later, darling
when you sat there naked, lighting
your cigarette on a moonbeam…
Seeing your full face,
bathed in deep

backlight and mild pain
(and how I could go on)
in this musicless room full
of your bright memories
and the words for
everything
except—

The Silence

I lay on my back in the field
watching the stars in the sky,
flickering like billions of fireflies, even more, a lot more
and the bottle of wine is empty
and I think of all this connecting us
with the fiber of time…

Thinking,
for how long?
And why,
why?

There is no exact answer
or at least one that we could understand.

And I'm thinking also:
what is the point of all this?

But then I remember what Issa said:

All the time I pray to Buddha
I keep on
killing mosquitoes.

Crime and Punishment

She said
something to me
without opening
her mouth –
then she made me
repeat it.

Short Prayer

I kneel as a child, but through the window
I look like a grown man.
Time's slipping away.
Let the women still smell of
warm loaves of bread.
Let the darkness always be beautiful,
indecipherable, unlike the light.
I close my eyes.
After that let me be turned into water;
a river hidden in the forest, which
can be found only by those who are
truly lost.

Alcohol

It is warm and cozy
here,
the night as Hydra
attacks the moon
above the sleeping
town and brings
the sedative for my
pupils,
my hand reaches to
the light bulb –
a lighthouse for
the ships of my dreams –
and then I,
black inside
as emptiness,
start to write
the endless letter
to my life
and
I sink right through
the words into the future,
into
the night.

Fast-slow Continuum

Jobless, illiterate, you walk
down the road, hands in pockets.
At the park you stop to look at
the kids and their mothers.
The sky is stretching beyond reason.
A sunlit book lies in the grass.

On This Earth

Resurrection of the morning summer light,
a tender wind's
parting the curtains,
something outside
calling her name,
calling gently
almost as a whisper
But who is going to
answer this time?
Certainly not the silence
coming from the cracked mirror—

We are living in this vacuum-like emptiness
of a nearly deserted city…

But there's a house surrounded by darkness and
a man's smoking by the window in delight.

The Darkness

You will find it everywhere after the sun hides
behind the hills and finally the moon appears,
carrying on its body holes and memories of
times gone by, when everything was still orderly
chaos. But the streets are different now. The single
incandescent lamp in the locked butcher shop shines
with bloody light and underneath it little chunks of meat
take part in a play about the human civilization.

Along the glittering window of the jewelry shop
a crippled beggar walks with his dog and he stops to
window shop with unseeing eyes. Across the street
is the bar and the last costumer inside sways like
a tree in a storm.

The museum is closed and the history inside it sleeps.
Kings and tribal chiefs have hidden their swords and
snore undisturbed right next to dinosaur's bones and
the saint, stoned to death. Only above him there is no light
and the dark feeling that there never was remains.

And Tomorrow

I return to the city of my childhood,
with the vast blue sky, snuggling with
the birds under the warm sun, to the smell
of vanishing darkness and beginning of
a new day, to the half-blind streets and
the boulevards full of beggars, mad men
and stray dogs, waiting for the night and
the next bottle or meal, to the church
full of wasted time and indecent promises,
to the faces on the sidewalks, empty of hope
and desire for something better, to the dark
Danube, which even Caesar wouldn't dare to
cross, to my youth, to the place where it all
began, to poverty and toil, to forgotten dreams
and aging, to already read books and bad poetry,
to misery, to hopelessness, to depression, to pain,
to the cemetery, which took from me everything
that I loved and will not give anything back,
to this whole city, an emanation of the end,
without new beginning, without resurrection,
to my old school with the crumbling walls and
still visible patches where the five-pointed stars,
the murals and the portraits of party leaders
used to stand for many, many long years,
to this country, which sold its soul a long time ago,
where I lived like an ostrich with my head in the sand,
to this place, this ghost of a city, where I was born to
write the last sentence before everything is gone forever.

Still

The sun is not ashamed to penetrate the tall window.
There's a fireplace with a dead fire. The grey color
loves the ashes. Yesterday's cat in rain is today's
warm smile under the table. Paint what you don't see,
which is me, looking at myself in the mirror, which is
an un-ploughed field of promise, full of ravens. Afternoon
filled with monochromatic light, seeping from the skies
of tomorrow–that's the unsolved color of music, which
we have to keep hidden inside our pockets. Memory
is red. If it bleeds, it bleeds. The clouds, hanging there,
are to the blank canvas what poetry is to the mind.

Simplified Philosophy

The ship inside the bottle
could be saved only
with some heavy hammer

and deep melancholy

The last of the seven
Russian nesting dolls
says *Mama* with an English
accent

All of the thousands still unread books
with their heavy silence never allowed me to do that

thing –

and at the end…

…it is just like Li Po said,
we are here with the mountain,
looking at each other, until
only the mountain
remains.

The Theory of Non-Relativity

The massless particle
which passes through vacuum
without encountering any resistance at all,
does not differ from the one
that does not pass at all

Loneliness is self-sufficient,
as they say and,
etc…

You're the last dark matter
from another outgoing night

but why don't you come with me, why
don't you come *in* me

to see that there's nothing
harder than
forgiveness

there's nothing

harder

I will fall asleep now just to wake up
in your life—

We'll not remember how we die,
just as we don't remember our birth.

Undisclosed

"Are we tired yet? Are you finished debating the blind
          who insist that light doesn't exist, and have proof of it?"
                                                    Franz Wright

Autumn light, illuminating the last bees
and even the darkness beyond
their darkness, which
 chaotically merges with the vanishing
summer cells filled with terminal
malignancy, while the night
as an endless snake crawls to the edge
 of the end and the sea comes and goes
whole eternity.
Night light, a door through which
I descent into the deep wells of your eyes,
there the memories are splashing and
nothing has changed and I'm pouring
myself into the open palms of your heart, where,
satiated, I will never again experience that thirst.
I believe again, everything's slowly approaching,
inconspicuous, beautiful, like rain falling in
the future, wetting the bones, going even deeper,
to the deep buried secret, and I'm lost again.
Church light, immense pain,
(the redemptive one):
we can be ourselves without anybody else telling us that,
our dirty halos, our candle light guiding us along the way,
there is nothing impossible
in this melting madness
of two gushing veins transforming into one;

time drips into the past—
everything I say is written on the paper of non-existence;
a child, you are only a child, I say to the sparrow
who makes holes in the sky
through which we can ascend.
The words fall and melt
like an ante-mortem snow, they melt
in last year's puddles of our eyes.
There, underground,
where I watched your laughter
hitting the walls, I'm looking at it now, still…
And I want,
when I will no longer be here,
to continue to exist with you, inside you;
that feeling of reversed irrevocability,
frozen between the ticks of the smiley face of
the clock, and you, guiding the time,
to hibernate throughout our winter
so we can meet again in the other
life.
Endless love light, this
I have hidden in my belly
but I know you can see it, feel it, red and
warm,
pouring over two hearts inside one warm body;
it will tell you, when I will no longer be able to,
what to do next
after the silence of darkness
and everything else hidden inside—
so many countless things, untold and forgotten
but no one should take the blame for it, just
sometimes everything gets lost
in this life but not here,
not now, not never.

Quietness

Emptiness is everything in this room.
Outside, the sky is not overflowing,
but pouring over the years.
What is the use of the numbers of time,
when she picks up the phone and says:

"Hello, please don't hang up. I want to
talk with someone."

But I am looking for spiders to build me
a clock out of silence,
crows for a poetry reading and rusty nails
for a different kind of farewell.

Shot in Brooklyn

The sun goes up.
They sit on the rusty fire escapes
and smoke reefers.
Laundry and sighs on the wires,
hung there like shot birds.
Everywhere is nowhere right here.
The sun goes down.
Their black faces are looking up
as the smoke is clearing over Manhattan.
40oz. of freedom is all they can afford.
And the night rolls up her dirty sleeves
singing silly songs of success.

Eclectic

The moment before
the moment of pain—
for example

her gaze becomes deep as a lake after the autumn rains,
full of drowned men.

We walk alone in the park and the leaves fall, fall…

Empty beer melancholy, we only have this life to live.

The Cross

In the darkness your white name
appears. It rises above my
world. The voice
whispers, the dark
thickens.
Small legs walk on
white land;
small hands pick up from the snow
a crown of barbed wire,
with absolutely nothing under it.

The Gentle Fish

My mama,
made of light, hazy stars and music,
swam gently through the chaos of the world.
At 66 she got tired of all this,
tired of the hard and muddy water;
she rose to the gleaming surface
and said she'll be home just before dark,
then she collapsed into the photo album
from where she gently smiles at me.

The Moment

The huge voice of Maria Callas filled
my little car like a stormy wind confined in
a matchbox in the middle of a wasted field.
But actually it was the summer highway outside

concrete Chicago. Or maybe I was inside *Tosca*,
or it may have been

Aida.

The road was spitting up scorching heat.
The midday traffic jam followed its sluggish
logic, the cars just stood there, facing the horizon.
Only my fingers moved in time with the great music.

And her voice was so hot that even
the air conditioner couldn't cool it down.
I lit up a cigarette and waited for everything to end -
this life, this world and this voice,

telling me about long dead things,
about lost love, about infidelity and war.
Finally, it was all over. I stubbed out the cigarette
and stared through the windshield at the setting

sun. I don't know how much time has passed.
Maybe a little, maybe a lot. Maybe I stayed
forever inside that moment that stretched out
endlessly with the last note, there, somewhere, together

with Maria.

II

Finding Things

This street is as lonely as it gets
and the same goes for the little girl
playing with dolls alone at the corner -
like a shadow in a dream -
between houses covered in twilight.

In this small and godforsaken town,
proud to have made the map,
in the middle of nowhere,
the sun is about to go down, but it sinks
so slowly, like a biscuit in a bucket of milk.

The grown ups are probably inside the houses
behind the drawn shades
or maybe in the graveyard
under the large stones
bloodied by the sunrise.

The night falls and everything disappears,
the houses, the prison, the hospital,
the school, the bar and the gas station
and even the small girl with her dolls
made of even deeper darkness.

Sunday Landscape

The blue yarn of summer days slowly

unravels, then comes the silky darkness;
her eyes in the mirror
half closed and waiting
for the life to come
but nobody knows what's
next, autumn or death, as we
sit in the classroom and
vainly waiting for the teacher
to come.

The world
is filled with people
who died only once.

Elusive Feeling

And I sink in the summer as the wind takes hold
of this sun-shaped box inside
my rib cage.

The green foliage is green with pain,
and I'm somewhere else.

Gods of light recline
in my eyes, but still
I can't find you
in the dark.

On through the endless night
the candle flickers -
a feeling descends
from the sky.

This dying—

I already forgot.

Sad is the Word

She really loves dogs and has five of them
and probably soon there will be even more.
When I ask her what about kids she just
shrugs. There's nothing more important for her
than those furry animals and I watch her watching
them running around the place, barking,
and I sit in the green chair under the dusty
sunlight, reading a book about China and how
they invented paper, the compass, gunpowder
and printing and how China often is considered
the longest continuous civilization, with some
historians marking 6000 B.C. as the dawn of
Chinese civilization. It also has the world's longest
continuously used written language.
But everything
ended between us when I told her that an estimated
10,000 dogs will be consumed for 10 days in
the Guangxi province during the Yulin festival,
but not because of hunger.

A Piece of Time

And the cup of coffee in my hand
and the sun warming up from above
and the concrete street with the people
and the iron tables crowding around me
and the tourists talking to each other
and the kids still half asleep and smiling
and the bird on the branch next to me
and the almost invisible thread in its beak
and the white clouds moving slowly
and your words when you said you would never come back
and I look at my watch that has stopped forever.

The Unknown

A small lizard on a boulder
looking straight at the sun's
scorching blaze. The day continues
to develop its endless narrative.
The doves in the distance listen
to the bells chiming deafly.
Somewhere in this world
a dictator issues an order for mass murder.

It's not just lies alone but simple truths as well.

The Hope

It was something like a whispered signing
directed at you

A love letter from the wind—

In this world there are people who are so lonely that
each hand reaching out to them is like a candle in
a dark cave.

All Love is Propaganda

It always comes unexpected –
truck in the rearview mirror on the highway;
the killer in a jump scare horror flick.
It is a block of concrete, a piece of mountain,
weighing on your shoulders,
moving slowly as a glacier in any direction it
chooses;
it never cuts like a knife deep in gut
but more like a paper on your finger tips
so you can suck on them in order to stop the flow,
it smiles at you through the distorted image
of thousands of opposite mirrors, faces.
Whenever you turn on the TV, the politician
is there, selling it –
lies about the present turning into lies about the future;
snapshots from an exotic place and your chances
to win a trip.
When you look up at the night sky and
all its majestic beauty at least you know
that all these stars have been dead for millions of years;
But I can say that sometimes there is a little bit
of truth in it,
like it was given to you by a dog, yes,
only the dog gives it
unconditionally,
unreservedly,
unquestioningly,
what it offers is for you forever,
and I guess this is a wonderful reassurance.

After the Bombing, Aleppo

Silence and moonlight
fills up each empty room

of the ruined city

just as the lava did with
the town of Pompeii;

happy children's voices
are laughing in the past.

Silence. Then somewhere a telephone
starts to ring and it rings

and rings and rings

        and rings—

Coffins

Their eternal darkness is equal for all of us,

but not like the condoms where one size fits all.

after Franz Wright

Under This

Under your skin there's another deeper layer of pale skin, more fragile.
Then I dived in it and swam to the large rock in the middle, which I saw from
the shore.
I did not drown. You dragged me out of your bloody sea before I could reach
my destination, your heart.
And yet I drowned, but it took me years to figure it out.

Uncertainty

Dimly lit room
with a flickering candle.

This small statuette of Buddha
on top of a thick book with
a cross on the cover.

Half-empty bottle
under half-empty heaven.

Not life,
but something else.

Reminder

You must always be—you always have to be yourself.
Each branch on the trees outside is different
from the rest, every leaf, too.
Each puddle of mud reflect the moon in
its own way. The fire in the stove is
never the same. The cold, too.

The world is ubiquitous, the world is fleeting.
Our old photos in the albums are
what we could have been in the past.
Our pains are alike, but whatever you've gone through,
there is always someone else who has suffered
much more than you.
Is not that right?

The sacred image of the saint on the mantle is silent.

Hey, do you remember me? – says the knife to the wound.

After Midnight

I love this city where when darkness falls and takes the houses
hostage until morning.
A night here is different from a night
above the sea, it's more civilized;
the small streetlamp outside
burns a hole in the flesh of the dark,
murmuring deep in its bones,
cradling it to sleep.
And then I live again;
the books on the shelves, hundreds
and hundreds of them, start to burn, just like this good
twilight in my room deserves,
every word I scribble in my notebook
starts to shine with a starry glow-
think of Van Gogh, think of Hopper-
and even if I drink a glass of water
it feels like it is full of promises for
a certain part of the night emptied of nightmares.
I look out the window and I see
a cab with squeamish passengers sleeping inside,
I see the dozing trees with their leaves
trembling slightly inside the wooden dreams
and I even can hear the music, coming from the sky,
where the night's scraping on its anthracite
violin.
And then I see the first hints of daybreak coming
from the horizon.
That's why I light a cigarette to force this horrible
darkness to take a step back.

Inside Look

Beauty is everywhere. Inside the day
of the night and the night of the day. Inside each fleeting
moment which is eternal. Inside everything in this world.
Inside the rose on the table, whose blood is redder
than life and whose life is more alive than everything
that ever lived. Inside the moon's sickle,
which bends even more and brings the winter's cold.
Inside all the little things that are dreaming huge
dreams of the eternal universe.

I remember when I looked through an electron microscope
and through its eye I could see where everything started
and where the chaos would begin again. And now I look
differently at everything around me: at the harsh wind,
which holds my hand like a big brother; at the memory
of the sea, which still remembers my shaking knees;
at the loneliness, which lives in all people who do not
believe in Heaven; at the daily sunset, blushing of
romantic sighs and clichés; at my beloved dead who
put me to sleep every night with lullabies that
sound like a dry river at the end of time…

…in the beauty of the flesh sinking in other flesh,
in the night which I'm sporting like a favorite
jacket, in my skin on which the constellations
are bruised, in the thread of life, tangled and
disentangled, tangled and disentangled…

Here and everywhere.

A man at some place sadly sips from a glass of
vodka.
Another man elsewhere happily burns a children's
book.

And I'm looking for myself inside the space.
And I'm looking for the space inside myself.

Here and nowhere.

Dark Off

I am still in the old dingy neighborhood,
waiting for the skies to turn into cashmere.
Ice-cream trucks play baroque symphony,
and the brown kids outside chase each other

in the dark with some whizzing lightsabers.
If I try to fry something I will eventually burn it,
and the avant-garde words from Cummings's "is 5"
crumble down on the wine stained carpet.

I attentively prowl the streets late at night,
stalking the shadows that are drawing nearer.
Concealing myself in the Serbian liquor store,
where the celluloid shop boy sells me bottles

full of canned laughter. It will be like this
until the end – eventually – no coke or grass,
just this indescribable mouth in my head,
lisping in my good ear "Times must pass".

III

The Cycle

On the street. I walk. On the sidewalk made of sidewalk. I walk fast and slow. In the night made of night. And stars of nothing. Dead. No noises. Just echoing steps. And time made of time. Black sky. Glowing firefly cigarette. Trees made of trees. Silence. Houses made of trees and stones. In my home. I drink vodka and water. Music. Vodka made of vodka and water made of time. Unending. Fifteen billion years. And I am still here. I drink fast and slow. News on the TV. War. Soldiers made of mothers and pain. Dying. I watch and I listen and I drink and I smoke and I breathe. Air made of air. And then I sleep and I dream. Nightmares made of nightmares. Blackness made of darkness. Finally dawn. Light and inhalation. And the beginning made of the end.

Afterlife

Let me visit the word
night now.

Three crows alight on the branches,
unusually silent and motionless,
and black as the word itself.

Everything else is gone…
Everything is not here…

So

is the light coming or going
after

the night.

In the Wilderness

In the room of the sleeping man
the air gets tattooed by darkness
and becomes raw, fragile.
The clock beats in sync with his
heartbeat.
Outside
the grass grows like a shadow
inside the dream of the horse sleeping
in the barn.
Dusty cobwebs in the corners
sway in the wind.
In the dark sky the sickle moon
burns like sin,
the next-door neighbor in his
tool shed builds a coffin out of light.

Swedish Sunset

In Memory of Tomas Tranströmer

A wintry, granite sun rises slowly over the milky clouds
of Runmarö. The color is not gray or white, but cold, cold.
It is warm inside the stones, shimmering on the shore,
like the heads of ancient Nordic children buried in

the sand up to their foreheads and licked by white light.
An unseen hand touches the backs of the mossy trees,
the island slowly settles in the horizon's edge where the sky
is a tangle of fading twilight and elapsed, echoing time.

Sometimes nature opens its eyes at noon and crawls out
among stones and greenery. And deep in the mountain:
the veins of the earth. The blood gushes through the years,
the eras and washes away the pain. Its heartbeat is a hammer on

the anvil of time, forging the eternal cells of oblivion.
The eagle rises high, locked in the fleeting moment, and carries
in its talons the sunset to the next life or to eternity.
And you are there, in the clouds, still writing the poetry

of now and forever.

Fading

Things all around fall into the night,
they darken, they ashen,

as the sun hides after a whole day with you,
as the sky breaks down from the midday heat,
as the dirt covers all unspoken sins,

and the night envelops even the candle flame
by the bed in the moonless room,

where we were young once
but now our dust is weighing on the wings of the moths,

and we reach out to catch the last light
left on our flesh

and our hands remain empty,
like a net in a fishless sea.

Afterglow

I had to do it—all of a sudden I had to eat the stars.
I was outside under the sky, drinking wine, eating bread—
But then, in the dark, I got things mixed up. I ate the stars.
Just when they tried to whisper something to me.

Then it became even darker. And I was completely alone.
Only the red drunken moon stayed with me. The empty bottle, too.
And the pain and my tears and the night. But at least I was fed.
My stomach was shining from the inside with dead time.

The Big Empty

A crow rubs his beak in the dust waiting for the storm –
time trickles in the bluest vase with the withered yellow rose;
  canned laughter after canned feelings in a world that only
partially
belong to us,
this shredded sky and the loneliness of the wolves hidden within
the debris of our love;
outside, the roots of the trees, like open mouths, drink
                from the yellowed pissed snow.

A Note on the Pillow

You live near the cemetery and
it is always dark at this place.
The shadows pull the stones together,
trapping them in a whirl of immobility;
I'll leave when the music's over
and when you promise me never again to point
that gun at the mirror.

Approaching the Truth

What is the German word for a man who loves
his wife and his three children, goes to work
without remorse and drinks only one beer on
Sunday? I don't know either. I just sit here and
watch the vast horizon, how the light ashen and
the day slowly turns into a dark night.

Sometimes I sit with a cup of tea in the morning,
watching the neighbors go to work, how they
kiss their wives and kids and pet the dog with
a smile on their faces. *Arbeit macht frei.* Then
I go to the back yard and I raise the flag again.
Birds fly freely in the bright sky. This is Hell.

Metaphysics for Beginners

There is a Hell,
said to me a shadowy figure on the street
at dusk
during my evening stroll

And what about Heaven then
There's got to be one
if Hell exists,
I asked

Nobody answered
He was gone
The sky darkened and the stars seeded the sky

I wanted to find him and ask him something else
but my owner tugged gently at the leash and we went
in another direction.

Obituaries in an East European Newspaper

I flip through the pages and they are always there,
with their eyes open as if they still want to see.
One of them is a serial rapist, shot by a police officer.
I've read about this a few days ago in the same newspaper.
Now I look at his eyes and I see that they look like piss-holes
in the snow, but even now they're still searching.
Then my wife came in the room naked and I threw the newspaper,
before he was able to catch a glimpse of her body.

Controversy

Sometimes we live and
sometimes we die inside this living

Sometimes the clocks stops and
the seconds peel like rotten oranges

And there are always premonitions
Death takes everything except our memories

My mother knits an endless sweater
with her bony fingers for knitting-needles

We must learn to live without pain

The red flowers on the nameless graves
open up like a rib cages

Through the gap in the sky a huge eye stares
at me without blinking

Where is you God
my father asks

*   *   *

I'm collecting baby pictures of Hitler, Stalin, Mao, Kim Il Sung,
Pol Pot, Leopold II,
Saddam to mix them with my baby pictures. We are ready to
worship whoever you
give us. On the screen the movie star is dying of thirst in the
desert, but in the cosmos
UY Scuti is the largest known star and it's 1700 times bigger than
our Sun. The actor
finds a well filled only with sand. There are more stars in our
Universe than there are grains
of sand on all the beaches on Earth, but a single grain of sand has
more atoms than there are stars in the Universe. These are mind
bogglingly huge numbers, right? Never mind! Just push the red
button, Mr. President.

Adagio

The morning brought the winter and the trees
whitened, like in a dream of an addict.
The only thing I can do in such whiteness
is to think of black things:
ravens, coffee and the insides of my head now,
where my thoughts are running like ants.
And when the sun rises, I will put my sunglasses
and I'll wait for the night.

My typewriter is chattering as the teeth of
a madman. With each keystroke they bite off
a piece of whiteness.
Darkness finally came.
The electrical power was off, the candles were
burned down to nubs, so I decided to
struck a match and light the sheet from the typewriter.
It burned out immediately, but for a moment lit up the room
and all the black faces at the windows.

Lament

I go out in the back yard with a beer
in my hand. In the dark
I look at the dark and at the indigo sky
above, empty of glittering stars
and satellites.
Load music starts from the house,
cutting the songs of the crickets in half
and the voice of the dead soprano
weighs like a gravestone in the air.
In the night's darkness I look into
nothing,
seek nothing,
just to lift this cold beer to my mouth
and listen to the deathly music.
Then the aria ends and the space
hangs listless as sheet and the silence
continues even more forcibly.
Several fireflies appear, out of the blue,
and I go inside so they can illuminate
the dark and sad space which my body occupied
until now.

Psalm

The Universe with all of its atomic tidiness is a bit
incomprehensible. Metaphysics too. But I like physics
more than the physicists. The world is full of geniuses
and some others. The world is strange, like a movie shot in
Technicolor, but there is too much red in it. Imagine
the Crusades, imagine the Inquisition, imagine all of it
until now. What if, like the fiction writers like to say,
time starts to flow in the other direction? Imagine Galileo
working with hexa-core processor, Henry VIII on Viagra,
Einstein sweating in a Chinese fireworks factory. That's why
I keep myself close to the agnosticism. This world
was screwed up before time was time, even before emptiness
gave any hints of vacuum. That's why I like the simple
things. For example, in a gas station in Arizona, in some
foreign language the American Indian at the counter tried
to explain to me how to pay for the gasoline. I asked him
in perfect Bulgarian whether he had read about the life of
Ambroise Vollard. At the end we understood each other
perfectly well in universal slang, and I continued west. Like
I said, I like the simple things. Now, I think about the grass
outside. About each leaf thirsty for a few drops
of water in this dried world, painted in blood. I think of
the world as an accordion, but I don't know how to dance
tarantella or polka. I think about all this pain for which there
is no vaccine. I have been in Silver City, New Mexico.
The city still scratches the memories of a gold rush. I've been
in the ghettos of New York. That's why I say that if we didn't
die we wouldn't care about the time. That's why I love
words. Everything is simple with words. But is there

anything worse than a creature who lives only to write poetry? Where are Ovid, Boileau, Dante? Is it still alive, Gilgamesh's aspiration to achieve immortality? Listen, we live and die. Listen, into the light of this cigarette you can find more life than the whole universe. That is enough.

Achilles

Empty white room with
three chairs in the middle
and nothing else.
There was a painting on the wall
but someone just took it.
Only the empty memory of it still
hangs there.
Like I said, there are three
chairs.
Identical, ordinary and
boring.
So which one am I?
What do you mean which one?
The chair that bleeds from
one of his legs, of course.

Ars Poetica

I am hammering this rusty nail
to the shaking tool-shed

and I am hoping to make it
stronger

and I thought I was a fool
for doing that

but I kept on with the hammer
anyway.

A Fake Memoir

Meanwhile,
I open the book

to read of nothing,
to read of me.

My face is stretched
from cover to cover

and the closer I get to the end,
the more my face wrinkles.

At the last page I can see the black dogs
sniffing the air.